MEGA BIKES

Created & produced by:
Picthall & Gunzi Limited
21A Widmore Road
Bromley
BR1 1RW
United Kingdom

Copyright © 2009 Picthall & Gunzi Limited

Design Manager: Paul Calver
Written and edited by: Louise Pritchard and Christiane Gunzi
Editorial assistant: Katy Rayner
Bikes consultant: Simon Bradley

Paperback ISBN **978-1-906572-31-0**

Reproduction in Singapore by Colourscan
Printed & bound in China by WKT Company Ltd

**Picthall & Gunzi would like to thank the following
companies and individuals for the use of their images:**
AJS-Regal Raptor® Motorcycles; American Honda Motor Co., Inc. -
Motorcycle Division; "Athol Williams The Flying Kiwi", courtesy of Stud
Racing – the fastest mph dragbike in the Southern Hemisphere Nov
2008; Bike Tours UK – www.biketours-uk.com; BLATA s.r.o; Brett Stevens
Racing; BRP Recreational Products UK Ltd; Chrysler UK Limited; Cobra
Motorcycles; Dave Jones at Santa Pod Raceway; Direct Bikes; F.Belley –
www.photof1.com; Honda Motor Europe; Intelligent Energy; Kawasaki;
Krazy Horse Custom Cycles; Marine Turbine Technologies; Mike Patrick
Photography – mike-patrick.com; Oz Trikes; Richard Doscher – Yuba City
Police Department; Simon Bradley – Motorbikes Today; Suzuki GB; Steve
Bailey, Gibbs Technologies; Thunder Media Service; Trike Zone; Triumph
Motorcycles Limited; www.maxmoto.co.uk; www.performance-art.co.uk;
www.wallysracephotos.com; www.wheelsracing.net; Yamaha Motors
Europe; Yamaha Motor Corporation, USA

CONTENTS

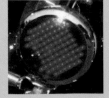

SPORTS BIKES

These exciting motorbikes are built to go fast, and there is no space for luggage. Sports bikes have a big engine and smooth bodywork that helps them to race along. Some sports bikes are used for stunts.

Buell bike

The windshield on this sports bike is smooth and curves backwards. The smooth shape is called 'streamlined'. A smooth bodywork means that the bike can go faster.

A stunt rider doing a 'wheelie' on a Triumph bike

curved windshield

Yamaha YZF-R6

Yamaha

This yellow Yamaha YZF-R6 has a 189-horsepower engine. This means that its engine has as much power as 189 horses. It can go at a speed of 187 miles an hour.

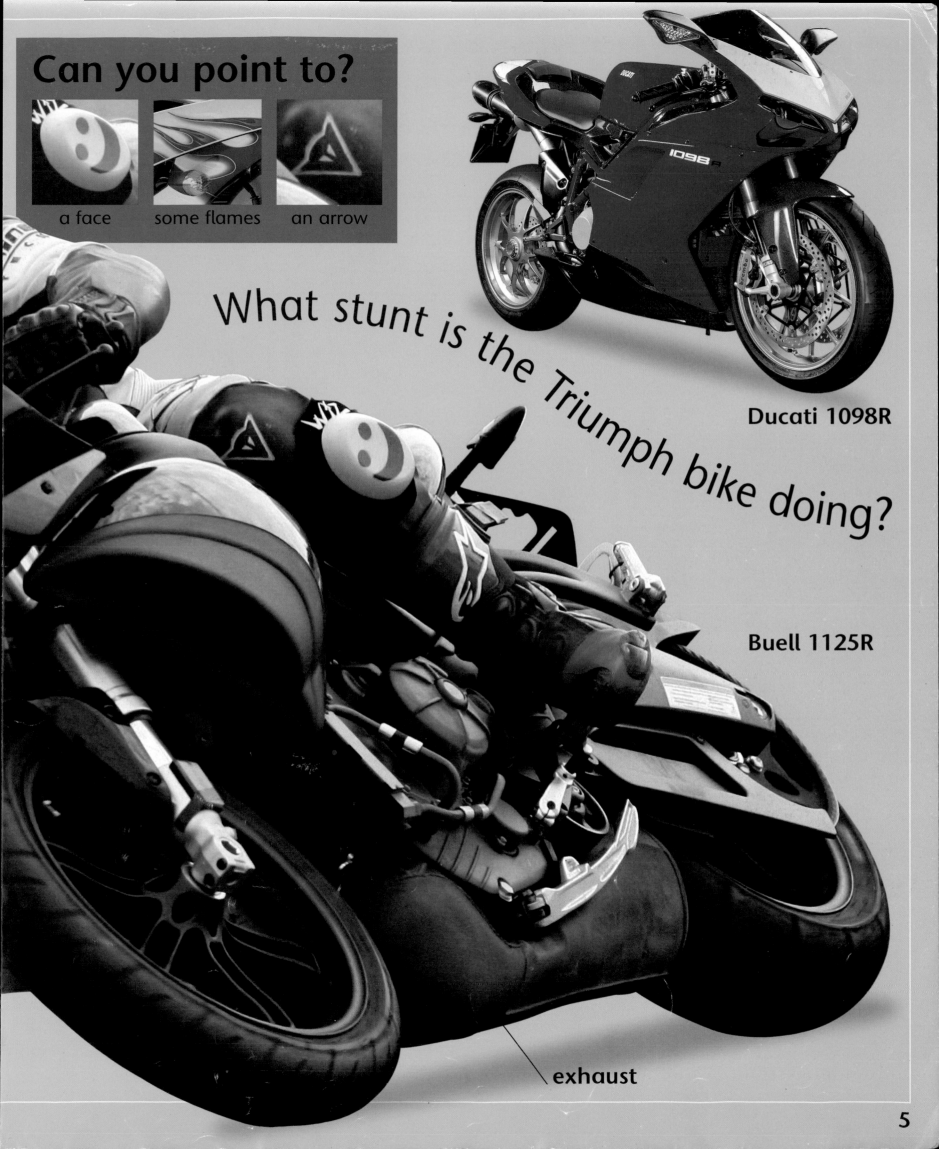

Can you point to?

a face some flames an arrow

What stunt is the Triumph bike doing?

Ducati 1098R

Buell 1125R

exhaust

5

TOURING BIKES

Some big motorbikes are made for driving long distances. These touring bikes are very comfortable. Many of them have heated seats and a CD player. They have room for a rider, a passenger and lots of luggage.

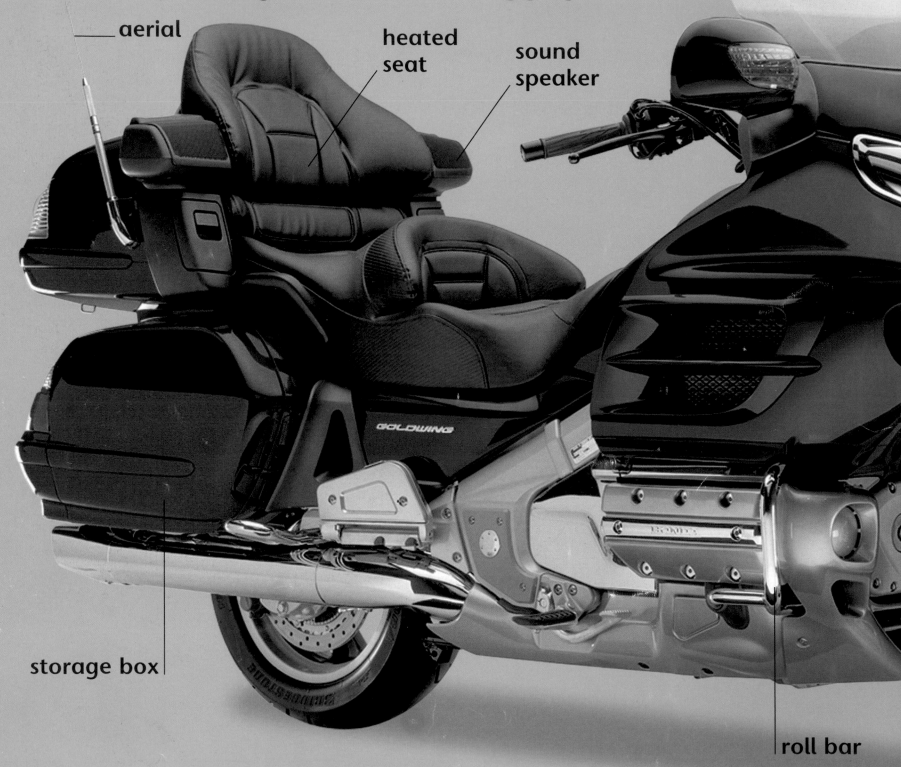

aerial

heated seat

sound speaker

storage box

roll bar

Honda Goldwing GL1800

Honda Goldwing's
dashboard

BMW touring bike

The BMW K1200 touring bike is very comfortable to ride, with a heated seat and heated handlebars. It has a 98-horsepower engine and it can travel at up to 122 miles an hour.

BMW K1200 LT

Where can you see an aerial?

Honda Goldwing

This smart bike is almost as comfortable as a car. Its seats are heated and have backrests. The bike also has an airbag and roll bars for safety. The luggage goes in storage boxes at the back and on the sides.

Front of Honda Goldwing

RACING BIKES

Motorbike races are fast and exciting. There are lots of types of racing bike. Some are tiny, and the motorbikes that do speedway races have no brakes! Motocross bikes are specially made to race on muddy tracks.

Motocross bikes racing in the mud

Minimoto racing

Speedway

A speedway race lasts less than one minute. Four or six riders race around a track four times. This race can be dangerous because the bikes have no brakes. To stop the engine the riders pull a cord attached to their wrist.

Minimoto

Children as young as six years old can take part in minimoto races. They ride very small bikes on go-kart tracks. Most of the bikes have a 4-horsepower engine.

Can you point to?

an oval

a cross

some stripes

Sidecars

In sidecar racing the driver and the passenger must work as a team. The sidecar rider leans from side to side to help steer the bike around the bends.

driver

sidecar

Sidecar racing

What kind of racing can children do?

Speedway racing

SUPER RACERS

These superbikes are big, noisy and powerful. They are heavy, but they are also fast because they have such big engines. The rider has to lean over to steer the bike around the bends.

Can you point to?

a moon

a number

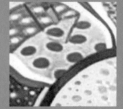
some spots

Yamaha MotoGP bike

This Yamaha bike is the fastest, most complicated and most expensive kind of racing bike. It can go at more than 200 miles an hour. This rider is the Italian, Valentino Rossi. He is the world's most successful MotoGP racer.

Who is the most successful MotoGP racer?

Honda Fireblade

Ducati 1098 F08

Superbike racing

Ducati superbike

The Ducati 1098 is a powerful superbike with a 160-horsepower engine. It is as fast as a MotoGP bike but is quite a lot heavier so the rider must be fit and strong to control it.

Yamaha YZF-M1

DRAG BIKES

In motorbike drag racing, two riders race each other along a short, straight track for a quarter of a mile. These amazing drag bikes travel so fast that they need a parachute to slow them down at the end of the race!

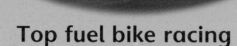

Top fuel bike racing

Pro stock bike

A popular type of racing is called 'pro stock' racing. This pro stock bike can go from 0 to 80 miles an hour in 1.5 seconds, and it reaches 170 miles an hour. It has special 'wheelie bars' at the back to stop it wobbling about as it whizzes along.

Top fuel bike

The fastest drag bikes are called 'top fuel' bikes. They use a special fuel called nitromethane and they are very noisy. Some can reach speeds of 337 miles an hour. This one has an 800-horsepower engine.

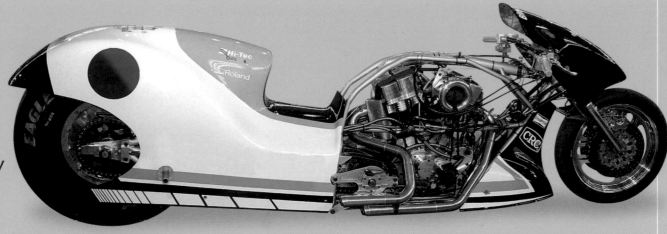

Top fuel bike

What is the fastest type of drag bike?

Pro stock bike

Can you point to?

some checks   a triangle   a star

rear 'wheelie bars'

PROSTAR

408

SCOOTERS

These fun motorbikes are easy to ride in busy places and are perfect for scooting around towns and cities. Most scooters have small wheels and a small engine, so they do not use up much fuel.

Honda scooter

Which scooter has three wheels?

Piaggio MP3

This Italian scooter has three wheels but it is still a motorbike. Two wheels at the front make it easy to ride. The Piaggio is a fast scooter, with a top speed of 90 miles an hour.

Piaggio MP3 250

Yamaha Giggle

Yamaha

This eco-friendly yellow scooter has chunky tyres that grip the road well. It is easy to ride and has a big boot under the seat. It is also cheap to run and easy to park.

sunroof

BMW C1

storage box

BMW

This BMW is a cross between a scooter and a car. You do not even have to wear a helmet to ride it in most countries. The scooter also has a sunroof, a reading light and some sound speakers.

STREET BIKES

Motorbikes are useful for getting around in towns and cities, where cars get stuck in traffic jams. Street bikes are specially designed to use in busy cities. Some of these bikes are very narrow, so they can get through the small gaps in the traffic.

Buell City X

This bike is small and easy to ride. It has the engine of a Harley sports bike so it can go as fast as 125 miles an hour. It has guards on the handlebars to protect the rider's hands.

Ducati
Monster S4R

Monster

This is a powerful new model of an old type of bike. This Monster S4R has a top speed of 150 miles an hour and is very noisy. That is probably why it is called 'Monster'!

Which of these bikes is the fastest?

Moto Guzzi
Stelvio

Moto Guzzi

This red Italian Moto Guzzi bike is only about one metre wide so it can weave in and out of city traffic. It can travel at up to 120 miles an hour. This bike has useful pockets for storing mobile phones and other things.

Can you point to?

some spokes

a light

some pipes

OFF-ROAD BIKES

These off-road bikes are good at crossing rivers, climbing mountain trails and steering through muddy forests. They have tough, chunky tyres to help them grip. Their wide handlebars make them easy to turn.

Honda

Trail bikes like this Honda are easy to drive over bumpy ground and they can cross shallow rivers. The knobbly tyres grip mud and stones well.

Honda crossing a river

Honda jumping over bumps

What are motocross race tracks made of?

Suzuki RM450

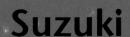

Suzuki

This is a Suzuki motocross bike. Motocross tracks are made of mud instead of tarmac and they have huge jumps. The bikes are very light so they can get over the big jumps.

helmet

mirror

mudguard

Yamaha trail bike

This Yamaha trail bike has big tyres to grip in the mud. The rider is standing up because it is easier to control the bike on rocky and slippery ground.

Yamaha
XT660R

CLASSIC BIKES

Some old, popular bikes are called 'classic' bikes. There are lots of different shapes and sizes. Some of these bikes are over 50 years old, and others are new bikes that are built to look like old ones.

Royal Enfield

The bike below is a copy of an old British bike. It has a sidecar, so the rider can take two passengers. The sidecar is made of fibreglass, which is light. This bike can cruise at 60 miles an hour.

Vespa

The first modern scooter was an Italian Vespa. This white scooter looks like the original one, but it has a powerful, modern engine.

Vespa PX 125

Triumph T140 Bonneville

indicator

spokes

Triumph

The British Triumph Bonneville bike was first made in 1959. It is named after the Bonneville Salt Flats in the USA. A Triumph bike beat the land speed record there in the 1950s.

Can you point to?

a wheel   a seat   some stripes

Harley-Davidson 'Fatboy'

windscreen

Royal Enfield 'Electra Jubilee'

Harley-Davidson

The big American motorbike above is called 'Fatboy' because it is so chunky. This famous motorbike has been used in many films.

sidecar

Which of these bikes was made in Italy?

QUAD BIKES

These four-wheeled motorbikes are also called ATVs (All Terrain Vehicles) because they can ride over all types of ground. Some even travel on water. They are fun to ride and do useful jobs.

Can you point to?

a diamond

some letters

a square

Which quad bike is used for farm work?

Quadski

The Quadski can go at 50 miles an hour on land and water. It is used by emergency services to rescue people from places that are difficult to reach.

Quadski on water

Quadski on land

huge tyre

Outlander 400 EFI

Outlander

This Outlander looks like the quad bikes that people race, but it is used for working on farms. It can carry a load of 135kg on its racks.

Midi-Quadard bike

front rack

handle

WORKING BIKES

Some motorbikes do important work. The police and ambulance services use them because they can travel very quickly through busy city streets. Bikes are also cheaper and better for the environment than cars.

Road King

This Harley Davidson motorbike is often used by traffic police. It is also used to escort important people or to clear traffic for emergency vehicles. It is strong enough to tow a broken-down lorry.

Taxi bike

In some countries, people use 'taxi' motorbikes to transport people around. A passenger pays a fare to the rider to get a ride across town.

Taxi bike

Honda Pan European Paramedic

Paramedic bike

Special nurses called paramedics use Honda motorbikes to get through traffic quickly. There is lots of storage space at the back of the bike so the paramedics can carry important medical supplies.

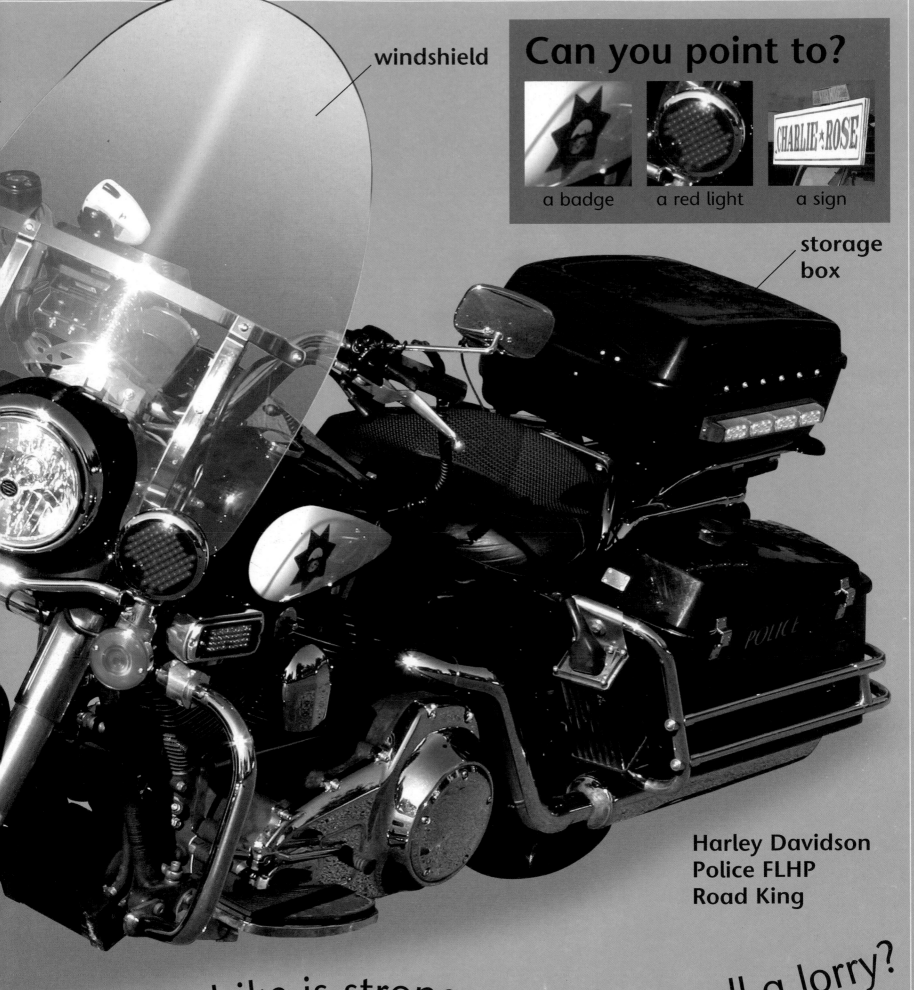

windshield

storage box

Harley Davidson
Police FLHP
Road King

Which bike is strong enough to pull a lorry?

TRIKES

A motorbike with three wheels is called a 'trike'. Some people like to ride trikes because they have two wheels at the back, which makes them easier to ride than a normal motorbike. Some trikes have long handlebars and big, comfortable seats!

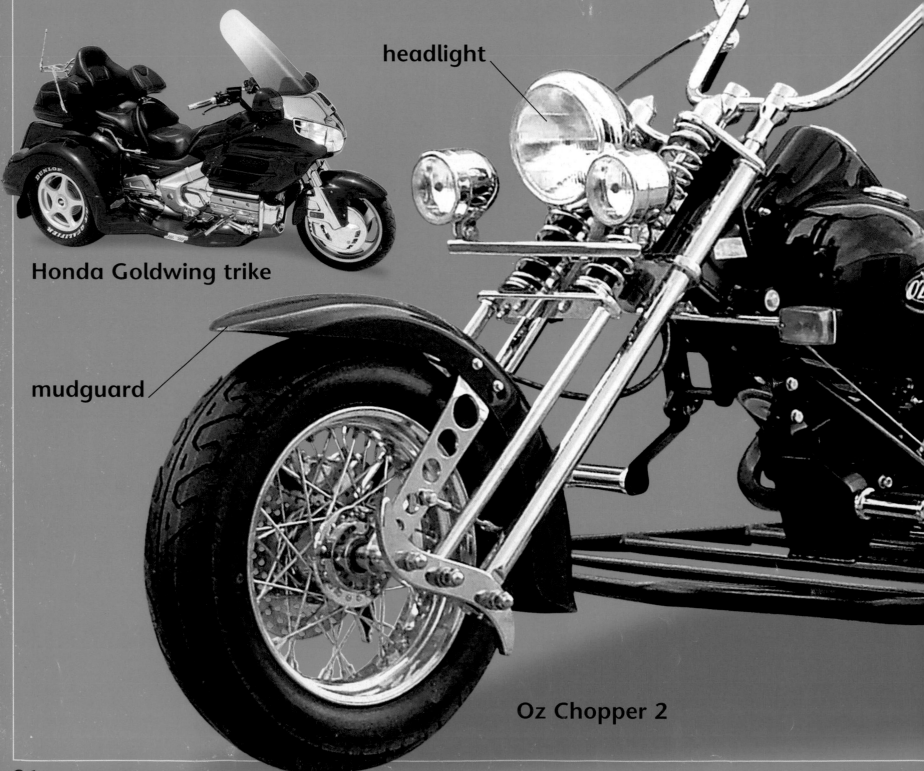

long handlebars

headlight

Honda Goldwing trike

mudguard

Oz Chopper 2

Chopper

The Oz Chopper 2 is a bit like a car. It has two large, comfortable seats and lots of space for luggage. The passenger seat is high up at the back, and it even has arm rests.

luggage on rack

rider's seat

huge chunky tyre

How many seats does the Oz Chopper 2 have?

AMAZING BIKES

Some bikes do not look like normal bikes. People build new bikes or change old ones to create their own weird and wonderful designs. These bikes are called custom bikes.

Can you point to?

some hexagons

a circle

some stripes

Snake

This amazing orange motorbike was made in Hungary. It took nine months to build and it is called 'Snake'. The design is very clever. It looks as if a snake has wrapped itself around the bike.

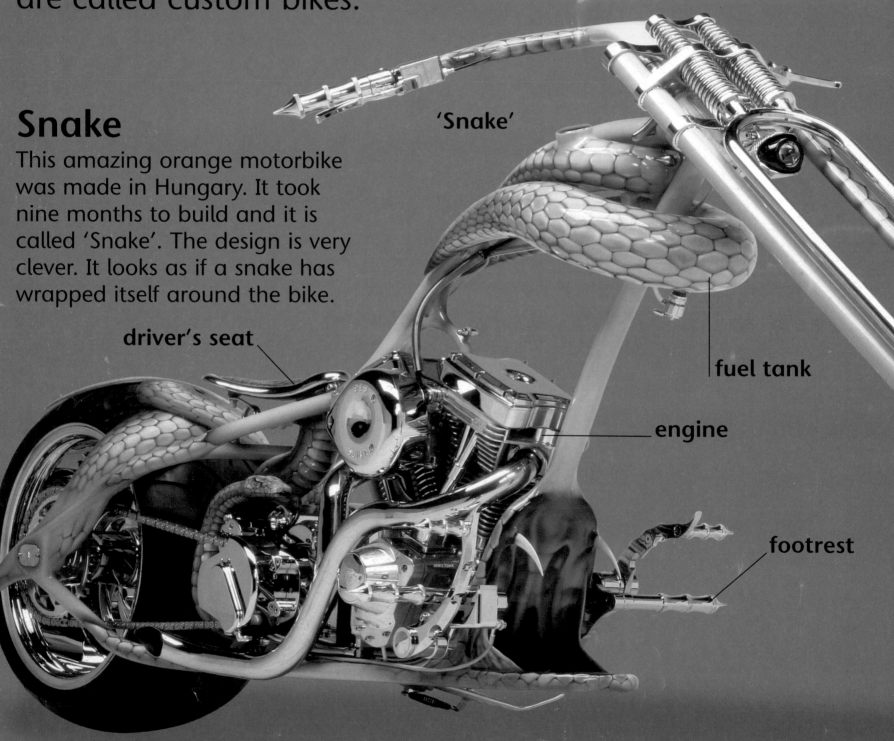

'Snake'

driver's seat

fuel tank

engine

footrest

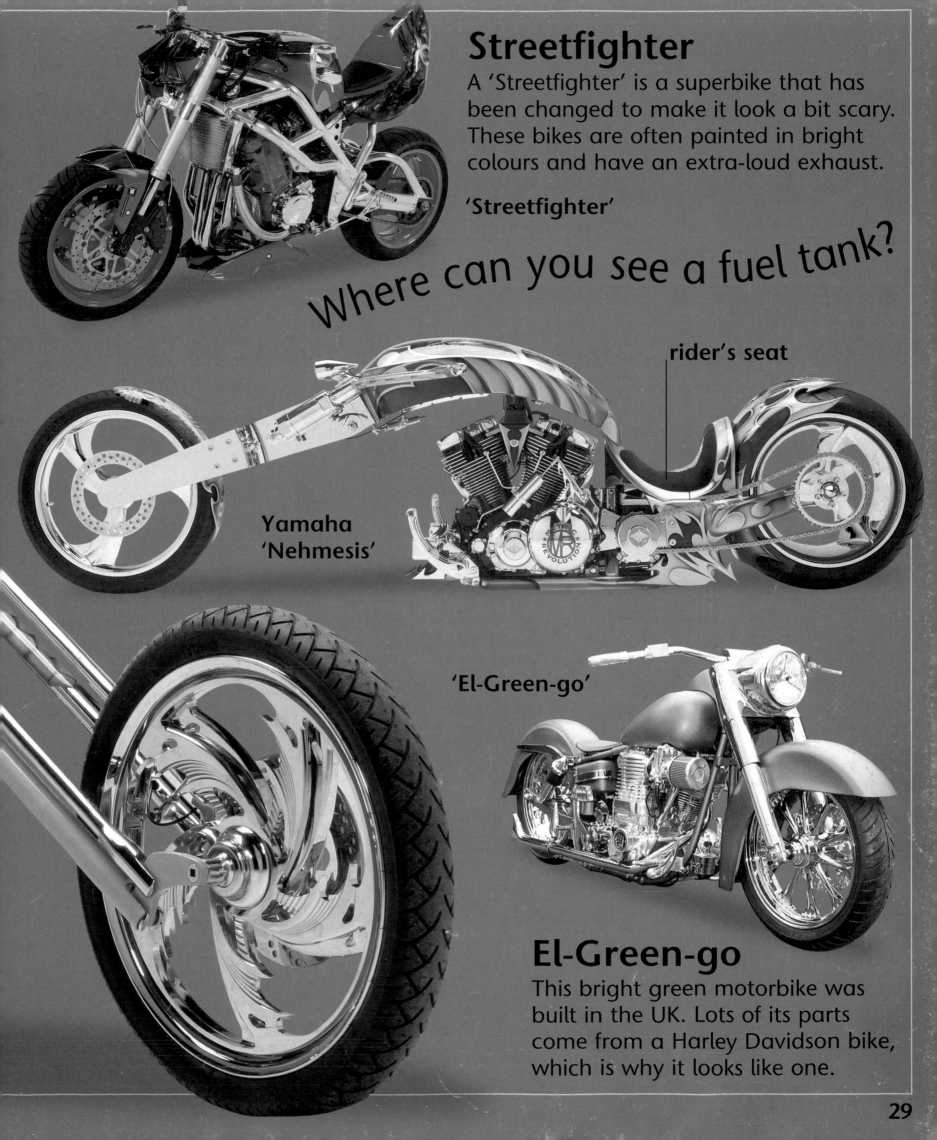

Streetfighter

A 'Streetfighter' is a superbike that has been changed to make it look a bit scary. These bikes are often painted in bright colours and have an extra-loud exhaust.

'Streetfighter'

Where can you see a fuel tank?

rider's seat

Yamaha 'Nehmesis'

'El-Green-go'

El-Green-go

This bright green motorbike was built in the UK. Lots of its parts come from a Harley Davidson bike, which is why it looks like one.

BIKES OF THE FUTURE

Bike designers often have new ideas, and their exciting designs are called 'concept' bikes. Many ideas are too expensive to make. But some designs do become real bikes, like this orange one with a jet engine!

MTT Y2K bike with a jet engine

Which bike uses hydrogen to make it go?

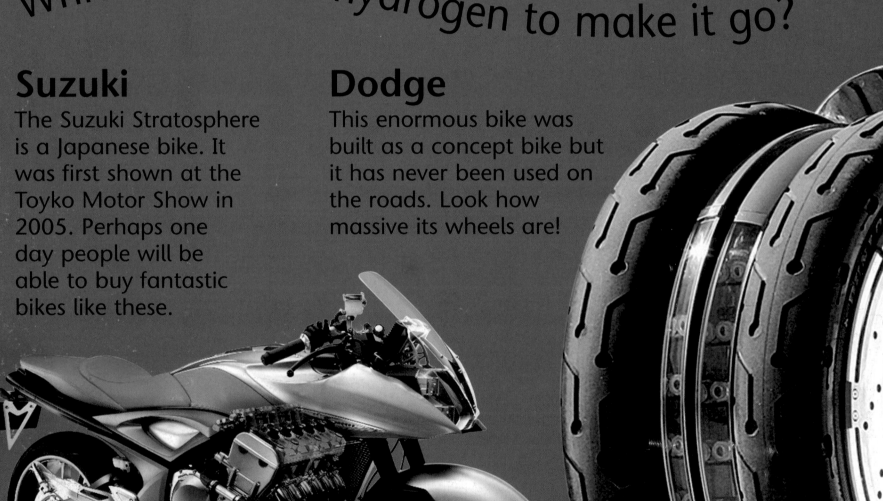

Suzuki

The Suzuki Stratosphere is a Japanese bike. It was first shown at the Toyko Motor Show in 2005. Perhaps one day people will be able to buy fantastic bikes like these.

Dodge

This enormous bike was built as a concept bike but it has never been used on the roads. Look how massive its wheels are!

Suzuki Stratosphere

ENV

This concept bike uses hydrogen instead of petrol. It gives off water vapour instead of fumes, so it is much better for the environment.

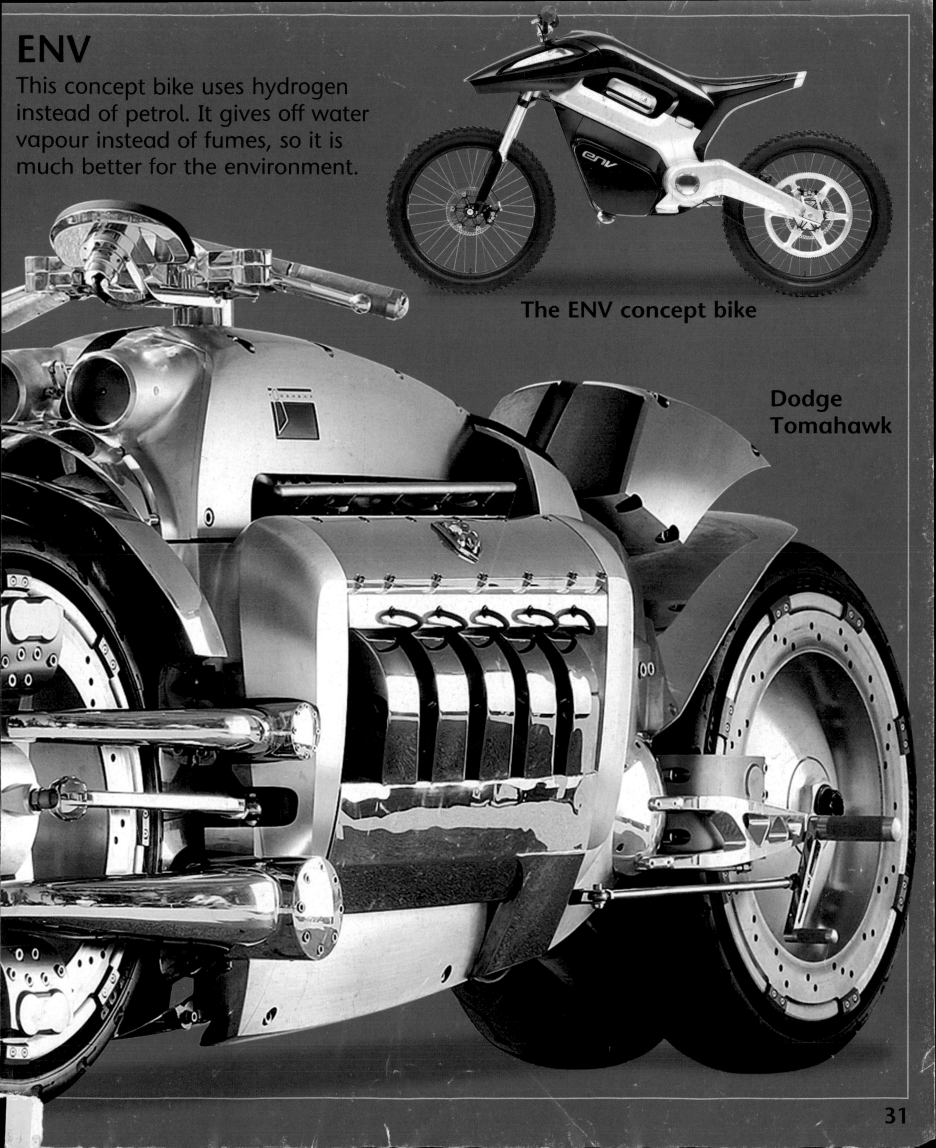

The ENV concept bike

Dodge Tomahawk

LET'S MATCH!

Can you find all the matching pairs on this page?

Which bike do you like best?

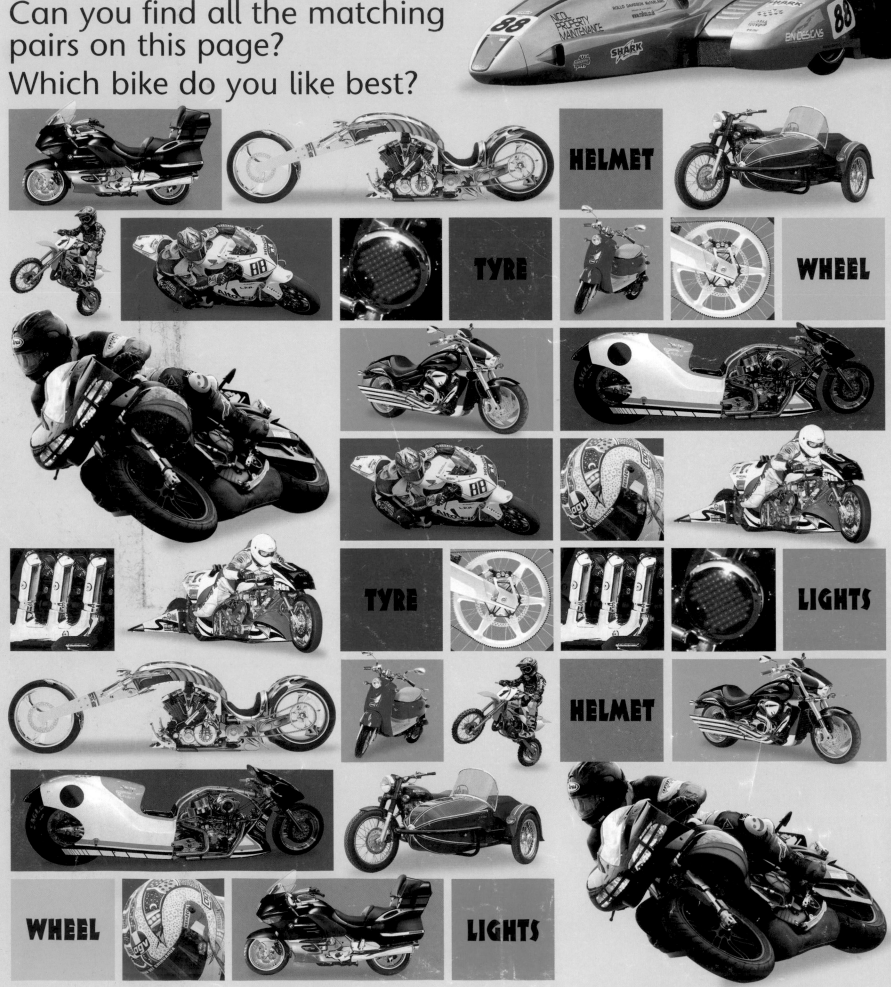

HELMET

TYRE

WHEEL

TYRE

LIGHTS

HELMET

WHEEL

LIGHTS